D1737078

Aullar, rugir, mugir y ladrar
Un libro sobre sonidos de animales

Molly Carroll
Jeanne Sturm

Howl, Growl, Mooo, Whooo
A Book of Animal Sounds

Rourke
Publishing LLC
Vero Beach, Florida 32964

LC 591.59
J 591.59
CAR

www.rourkepublishing.com

PHOTO CREDITS: © Cliff Parnell: Cover; © Larysa Dodz: Title Page; © Tessa van Riemsdijk: page 3; © John Pitcher: page 4, 6; © Lynn Stone: page 5, 9, 15, 24; © Davina Graham: page 7, 24; © AtWaG: page8; © Jerry Mayo: page 10; © Steve McSweeny: page 11, 23; © Tomasz Pietryszek: page 12; © Heinrich Volschenk: page 13, 23; © Nicholas Homrich: page 14; © Eric Isselée: page 16, 18; © Arkadiusz Stachowski: page 17, 24; © Alexander Hafeman: page 19, 23; © David Hernandez: page 20; © Nicole S. Young: page 21

Editor: Meg Greve and Kelli Hicks

Cover design by: Renee Brady

Interior design by: Tara Raymo

Spanish Editorial Services by Cambridge BrickHouse, Inc.   www.cambridgebh.com

Library of Congress Cataloging-in-Publication Data

Carroll, Molly.
  Howl, growl, mooo, whooo, a book of animal sounds / Molly Carroll, Jeanne Sturm.
      p. cm. -- (My first discovery library)
  ISBN 978-1-60472-531-5 (hardcover)
  ISBN 978-1-60472-508-7 (hardcover bilingual)
 1. Animal sounds--Juvenile literature. I. Sturm, Jeanne. II. Title.
  QL765.C357 2009b
  591.59'4--dc22

                    2008025169

Printed in the USA

CG/CG

Rourke Publishing

www.rourkepublishing.com – rourke@rourkepublishing.com
Post Office Box 3328, Vero Beach, FL 32964

Los animales hacen muchos sonidos.

Animals make many sounds.

El lobo aúlla,

The wolf howls,

HooooooWW

4

y la pantera ruge.

and the panther growls.

GRRRRG

OWWL

7

La vaca muge: "Muuuu",

The cow says, "Moooo,"

OOOO

y el búho ulula: "Uuhh-uuhh".

and the owl says, "Whoo-Whoo."

Whooo

La abeja zumba: "Bzzz bzzz",

The bee says, "Buzz Buzz,"

BUZZZZ

y el perro ladra: "Guau, guau".

and the dog says, "Ruff Ruff."

Ruff

Ruff

Ruff

La oveja bala: "Baa, baa",

The sheep says, "Baa Baa,"

BAAAa

Baaaaa

y el chivo berrea: "Beee".

and the goat says, "Maa."

Maaa

aaaaaaa

Ahora dinos, ¿qué sonidos haces tú?

Now tell us, what noises do you make?

Glosario / Glossary

abeja: La abeja es un insecto que vuela y tiene un cuerpo peludo y cuatro alas. Las abejas coleccionan el polen para hacer la miel. Las abejas usan sus lenguas largas para sacar el néctar de las flores.

bee (BEE): The bee is a flying insect with a hairy body and four wings. Bees collect pollen to make honey. Bees use their long tongues to get nectar from flowers.

búho: El búho es un animal con ojos grandes, un pico curvado y garras afiladas. Los búhos cazan de noche. Comen ratones y otros animales pequeños.

owl (OUL): The owl is a bird with large eyes, a hooked beak, and sharp claws. Owls hunt at night. They eat mice and other small animals.

chivo: El chivo es un animal con pezuñas, cuernos y barba. Los chivos se crían por su leche, lana y carne. Podemos beber la leche de los chivos o podemos usarla para hacer mantequilla y queso.

goat (GOHT): The goat is an animal with hooves, horns, and a beard. Goats are raised for their milk, wool, and meat. We can drink the milk from a goat, or we can use it to make butter and cheese.

lobo: El lobo es un animal salvaje, pariente de los perros, coyotes y zorros. Los lobos cazan con otros lobos en manadas, o grupos.

wolf (wulf): The wolf is a wild animal that is related to dogs, coyotes, and foxes. Wolves hunt with other wolves in packs, or groups.

oveja: La oveja es un animal con pezuñas, cuernos y pelo rizado. Las ovejas se crían en granjas. Las ovejas nos proveen lana y carne.

sheep (SHEEP): The sheep is an animal with hooves, horns, and curly hair. Sheep are raised on farms. Sheep give us wool and meat.

pantera: La pantera es un leopardo grande con pelo marrón o negro. A las panteras también se les llaman pumas o gatos monteses.

panther (PAN-thur): The panther is a large leopard with brown or black fur. Panthers are also called cougars or mountain lions.

Índice Index

Lecturas adicionales / Further Reading

Elliott, David. *On the Farm*. Candlewick Press, 2008.

Van Leeuwen, Jean, and Ann Schweninger. *Amanda Pig and the Really Hot Day*. Puffin, 2007.

Meister, Cari and Amy Young. *My Pony Jack at the Horse Show*. Viking, 2006.

Sitios web / Websites

www.seaworld.org/animal-info/sound-library/index.htm
www.alphabet-soup.net/farm/farm.html
www.naturepark.com/sound1.htm

Sobre las autoras / About the Authors

La familia de Molly Carroll tiene un gato anaranjado que suele decir: "Miau".

Molly Carroll's family has an orange cat that frequently says, "Meow."

Jeanne Sturm y su familia viven en Florida, con un perrito muy activo, dos conejos amistosos y muchos peces coloridos.

Jeanne Sturm and her family live in Florida, along with a very active dog, two friendly rabbits, and many colorful fish.